Table of Contents:

About this book

One day at a large book store, I started looking for a simple book that summarized the best training tips into easily read and actionable pieces of advice. But after a long search, I found that if a runner wanted a quick read on running's "best practices," they were out of luck. I decided to change that and write this book.

That's what you're reading right now: 14 years of running lessons distilled into 102 (I know, more than you asked for!) easily implemented training tips. Use them to inform your training, lead a healthier lifestyle, prevent injuries, and get faster.

You'll find lessons about performance improvement, racing, diet, and injury prevention. No matter how experienced you are as a runner, you'll learn something to improve your training and reach your goals.

Keep in mind that every piece of advice in this book has been tested on me, with the runners I coach, or is being used among the top runners in the country at the elite level. None of this is pure theory. Many of these strategies helped me run 2:39 in the marathon (over 5 minutes faster than my previous race) and stay injury-free for three years and counting.

If that sounds like something you'd like to do yourself, you have the right book! Running is a journey and you'll continue learning about it for years to come. I'm just like you - I remember being a total rookie like it was yesterday and now my understanding of training helps me coach other runners to achieve their best. I've been on both sides of the fence.

If you read this book and implement everything you learn, I can guarantee that you'll become a better runner, improve your race times, and prevent more injuries. It doesn't matter if you're a total beginner or a veteran, I've been there and can show you how to improve.

But before we start I need you to do something for me. Connect with me on facebook at facebook.com/strengthrunning - I'd love to stay in touch and learn more about your running.

Thanks again for choosing this guide on better running - now get a pen and get ready to take some notes!

Workouts, Races, and Performance

This section is where you'll find the "running" advice - from workouts and races to strategies that help you run faster. Most running books deal with this subject - and only this subject. What could be an entire book is distilled into the most important actionable lessons for you to start using right away.

1. Hill workouts don't have to be repetitions.
Every coach I know encourages a good hill workout. And for good reason - they build leg strength, help prevent injuries when done correctly, and give you a great aerobic stimulus (i.e., help you develop endurance). But they shouldn't be the only hills you're running.

In addition to a hill repetition workout, you can also run 1-2 "rollercoaster runs" throughout the week. These are simply easy or moderate paced distance runs that are run on hilly terrain. Don't run fast on the uphills and downhills; just keep your effort constant for the entire run. Including 2-8 (or more!) hills of different lengths and grades during a typical run will help you build resilience and improve your running economy. Just limit your hilly days to 2-3 per week to ensure you're recovering properly.

2. Start doing strides 2-3 times every week.
It's incredible how many runners just aren't doing strides on a regular basis - and in fact, many don't even know what they are.

Strides are simply 20-30 second accelerations done after an easy run. They can be done almost anywhere - a parking lot (just be careful!), your street, a long driveway, or a field. Start by running at an easy pace, and then gradually get faster until you're at about 95% of your maximum effort. Hold that for about 2-3 seconds, and then gradually slow to a stop. That's one stride.

Take 30 seconds to a full minute of walking or standing rest in between each stride Start with four and increase to six or eight strides. Keep in mind that strides are relatively short, so while they're fast (well, for a *few* seconds), they shouldn't be hard at all - they're fun!

3. Better yet, do some strides barefoot.
For more foot and lower leg strength, you can run some or all of your strides barefoot. Before you do, make sure that you have a good place to run them;

you can't do them anywhere.

Barefoot strides are best done on a well-manicured or synthetic turf field where you know the surface is smooth and free of small rocks, sticks, or glass. Start by doing 1-2 strides barefoot and then take a few days to see how your feet feel. The next time you can increase to 2-4 strides.

Running strides barefoot not only helps you develop lower leg strength, but you're also improving your running economy and developing more efficient form. Win-win!

4. Sprint uphill!
Hill sprints are a valuable tool in any distance runner's toolbox. These are 8-10 second maximum intensity sprints up a steep hill, with a full 1-2 minutes of walking in between each sprint. They help you develop neuromuscular efficiency, injury resistance, better running economy, and leg power.

Start with just two reps and always do your first one at about 95% effort to warm up. You'll initially be sore, but after 3-4 days you'll be ready for your next session. You can increase by 1-2 reps until you reach 6-10 total.

Remember to always run easy before doing hill sprints. You need to be properly warmed up. Hill sprints are like running-specific weight lifting - perfect for developing the power you need to run fast.

5. Be a "core whore."
My wife jokes that I'm a core whore because I make a 15-20 minute core session an almost daily part of my post-run routine. You don't necessarily need to do a core workout every day, but start doing one about 3 times per week and you'll start seeing real results.

Focus on whole body exercises that you can do anywhere, like pushups, planks, bridges, and lunges. An effective general strength routine that I used frequently is the Standard Core Routine: http://strengthrunning.com/2012/01/the-standard-core-routine-video-demonstration/.

A more strength oriented workout is the ITB Rehab Routine: http://strengthrunning.com/2011/02/the-itb-rehab-routine-video-demonstration/. The ITB Rehab Routine is focused on glute and hip strength -

two areas that are particularly weak among most distance runners - and is great for overall injury prevention, not just for those who suffer from Illiotibial Band Syndrome.

6. Core is about more than your abs.
If you design your own core workout, keep in mind that your core is about much more than just your ab muscles. Include exercises that engage your lower back, hips, and glutes - all of these muscles are important to stabilizing your body when you're running.

Even if you're in the gym lifting weights, you're using your core muscles. Exercises like the squat, dead lift, and weighted lunge all work your core muscles and help stabilize your upper body. Just don't limit yourself to sit-ups every day!

7. Get stronger - in the gym or at home.
Once or twice per week you should focus on more than just your core muscles. Overall body strength is important and you should work on it regularly. Whether you're in the gym or doing bodyweight exercises at home, general strength can help you recover faster from your faster workouts and improve your running form.

My favorite exercises in the gym include squats, dead lifts, weighted lunges, bench press, pull ups, military press, chin ups, and dips. If you're working out at home, you can do pushups, lunges, dead lifts (pick up a paint can or anything heavy but stable), side and front planks.

8. Don't be a one trick pony when you're getting strong.
Make sure your core and strength workouts challenge your body in all three planes of motion: front and back, lateral, and rotational. Since running is all front and back motion, it's important to move in different planes of motion to stay athletic and improve your injury resistance.

Here are a few exercises that help you do this:

1. Lunge forward and rotate your trunk to the side and back as you lunge

2. Side plank

3. Side leg lifts

4. Side lunges

5. Hay bales with a medicine ball (squat down with a med ball, then as you raise up you lift the ball up and to your side. Rotate your trunk and watch the ball as you rotate it to your side.)

Running creates imbalances because it's a repetitive movement in one plane of motion. Counteract those imbalances with exercises in multiple planes of movement to stay healthy.

9. Run different types of long runs.

Long runs don't have to be the same pace. In fact, you can squeeze even more fitness out of your long runs by varying the terrain and pace that you run in the later miles.

Three of my favorite types of long run variations include:

· Hilly long runs: run several long hills in the final 2-5 miles or run one long hill of 5-10 minutes in the final 1-2 miles of your run.

· Long runs with surges: With 1-2 miles left in your long run, start a short fartlek workout. My favorites include 8 x 30 seconds at your 10k pace with a 1-2 minute jogging recovery or 6 x 1 minute at your tempo pace with a 1-2 minute jogging recovery.

· Progressions: In the final 2-5 miles of your long run, gradually pick up the pace so you end your run at your tempo or 10k pace. This is definitely an advanced type of workout, but it'll help you gain even more endurance as you teach your body to run fast when it's tired.

These are slightly more advanced versions of the standard long run, so progress intelligently and start with hills, then do a fartlek long run, and finally end with the progression.

10. Make sure you do a warm-down after *every* run.

Do *something* after you run – either body weight strength exercises, core work, or a flexibility work; it will dramatically lower your injury risk by increasing your functional flexibility and general strength. Just 5-10 minutes of easy or moderate exercises done in your living room or front lawn (don't mind your laughing neighbors) is all you need.

This type of work helps you properly warm-down from a running workout and can help make you a more efficient runner (plus cut down on pesky overuse injuries). For many runners, it might be best to cut back on your run so you can include more strength exercises after you finish. If you're consistently injured, this could help you stay healthy.

11. Run a race you've never run before

Too often we get stuck in a rut of only running 5k's or 10k's. It's time to break out and discover other races! Less common distances like 8k (about 5 miles) and 10 miles can help you break out of a funk - plus, if you've never run these distances you'll automatically get a shiny new PR!

Distance isn't the only variable you can play with - try running a track or cross country race to get off the road and try something really new. The speed of the track or the strength required by a cross country race can help you discover what you're good at.

And if you're truly bored with "just" a running race, then try a race with obstacles like a Warrior Dash or Tough Mudder. Make sure you're also doing enough strength exercises to be able to confidently complete the many obstacles you'll be faced with during the race!

12. Stick to basic exercises in the gym.

The classic movements are often the most effective. When you're in the weight room, focus on compound, multi-joint exercises like pull-ups, dead lifts, squats, lunges, bench presses, military presses, and chin-ups.

Instead of training muscles, you're training *movements* with these exercises. They're more effective at developing whole-body, functional strength that will carry over into your running than targeted exercises like bicep curls - which are useful mostly for bodybuilders.

13. When you lift, lift *heavy*.

You train for endurance when you're out running. But when you're in the gym, you shouldn't lift low weight for high reps - you need to lift for *strength* in the gym.

For all of your gym exercises (especially the leg exercises like squats and dead lifts), aim to complete 4-6 reps for 3 sets. It should be difficult for you to complete the last rep. And don't worry about gaining "mass" - runners run too much to gain a ton of muscle weight. If anything, you'll just improve your body composition!

14. Become a midfoot or forefoot striker.

Running as efficiently as possible is going to help you run faster with less effort. An added benefit is that you'll reduce the impact shocks that your legs experience with every foot strike and reduce your chance of injury.

One of the best ways to do this is to adjust how you run so that your foot strikes on your midfoot (the middle of your foot). Think of landing with a flat foot instead of angling your toes up and landing on your heel.

Now with that said, keep in mind that heel striking isn't inherently bad - in fact, 2009 New York City Marathon winner Meb Keflezighi is a slight heel striker. If you've been running for years or are a more competitive runner, then don't try to adjust your form too much. Your body has learned the best way for it to run already through a lot of practice.

But if you're a new runner, some slight changes to your form can help you run easier, faster, and with fewer injuries.

15. Don't over-stride when you run.

Over-striding means landing with your foot significantly in front of your body. Over-striders are usually aggressive heel strikers and put more stress on their legs than those who don't over-stride.

Instead, make sure your feet are landing underneath your center of mass. Try to envision just "putting your foot down" underneath your body rather than reaching out with your foot. This simple cue will help you run more efficiently with a more compact stride.

16. Increase your cadence to 180 steps per minute.

Now, there's nothing inherently "magic" about 180 steps per minute. There's no ideal stride rate. But an approximate stride rate of 180 will help alleviate many inefficiencies in your running form.

A quicker cadence will help reduce impact forces and your chance of injury. It will also dramatically lower the chance that you're over-striding.

There are a lot of running form articles that will recommend you focus on being a midfoot striker. Sure, this is important (and I recommend it as well), but the best thing you can do to improve your form is by taking quicker steps. Aim for at least 170 but ideally you'll be somewhere around 180 steps per minute.

17. Bend from the ankles, not the waist.

Many runners try to perfect that forward lean they've heard about so often. And it's true - runners should have a very slight forward lean. But where most runners get it wrong is that they lean *from the waist*, instead of from the ankles. Leaning from the waist puts a lot of added stress on your legs and can easily result in an injury if you continue with that form.

Leaning forward from the ankles ensures that you use a little bit of gravity when you run. You might find that you're engaging your glutes more than you used to - that's normal. In a proper running stride, the glutes provide stabilization and help you remain upright, especially when you're leaning from the ankles.

18. Consistency, consistency, consistency!

Running well takes months and years of diligent work. Unfortunately, there's no short-term fix or "get fast quick" plan out there. Distance running is a long-term sport and it takes the top athletes *years* - sometimes decades - to reach their genetic potential.

Remember that what you run today impacts what you're able to do next week, which impacts what you can do next month, etc. Consistency is king and you'll often get better results by adding a little bit of running for a few months than trying to jump up your mileage over just a few weeks. Small changes, made over a long period of time, will ultimately help you be a better runner.

19. Don't blindly follow the 10% Rule.

The 10% Rule states that you should only increase your mileage by 10% or less per week. But this "rule" is too simplistic for most runners and you should modify it for your own situation. Listen to your body because sometimes 10% will be aggressive, while other times you'll be ready for more.

Figure out your "mileage baseline" - the number of weekly miles you're comfortable at. You can aggressively increase your mileage to this baseline but then you should be more conservative once you're at or above your baseline. It's also a good idea to hold your mileage at the same level for 2-3 weeks before increasing it to ensure your body is fully adapted to the higher workload.

20. Don't burn the candle from both ends.

This is a rule I learned the hard way in college. If you're partying too much, eating like crap, or not sleeping enough then you can't train at your normal level. You'll need to cut back on your training to allow your body to recover from your non-running extracurricular activities.

When you're sacrificing a healthy lifestyle at the same time as running and working out a lot, it's a surefire recipe for injury.

21. Once a week, run something random.

Variety is the spice of life - and also the spice of a good training plan. Experiment with your program and explore a new trail, a hill workout instead of an interval workout, a fartlek instead of a tempo, or running with a friend.

Alternate your shoes with a pair of minimalist trainers. Run a few faster surges at the end of your long run or end your tempo uphill for once. These seemingly minor variations in your training keep you fresh both physically and mentally. They'll also help you reduce injuries as you're not stressing your body in the same few ways throughout your entire training cycle.

22. Learn to love negative splits.

Running a negative split simply means running the last half faster than the first. You should negative split most of your distance runs, workouts, and races if you can.

Negative splitting runs during training will increase your confidence to do it during a race - when time really counts. You also get a better aerobic stimulus (as in, more endurance!) when you teach your body to run faster later in a run when you're already tired.

It's easiest to do these types of workouts on out-and-back runs where you can time each half exactly. Any workout on the track lends itself well to negative splits since you can monitor each interval time to the second. Have fun with it!

23. Race a distance you've never run before.
What's so special about running a new distance? First, you'll get an automatic PR! Setting a benchmark in a new distance gives you an entirely new race distance to think about and plan for.

But more importantly, training for a new race distance means your training is going to be slightly different. If it's a longer race, you'll likely need more challenging long runs and longer workouts. For shorter races, you'll need the opposite: faster workouts and an emphasis on developing your speed.

Aside from the physical benefits of racing a new distance, this is another example of a "small win" - it will give you a PR and a whole new race experience.

24. Never try something new on race day.
This is a common problem among new runners or those who don't race frequently. No matter your running history, there shouldn't be any surprises on race day. Your race day routine should be exactly that - routine.

This means your shoes, in-race fueling, clothing, breakfast, and hydration should all be things that you've experimented with during day to day training. Some runners can't eat dairy before they run, so cereal is out. Don't try a wacky breakfast!

For longer or more serious races, this rule also applies to your dinner the night before a race. The last thing you want is to eat something that upsets your stomach the next morning.

25. A distance race can't be won in the first minute, but it can be lost.
Watch any big race and you'll see a few runners go out in a fast sprint - and then slow down dramatically. These runners won't run their best and will probably feel terrible for the remainder of the race.

When you sprint at the very start of a race you'll dig a hole you can't run out of. Instead, run your goal pace from the very start. And if you feel good, you could negative split the end of the race. Starting a race faster than your goal pace is an advanced pacing strategy and should only be attempted by faster runners who know what their bodies can handle.

26. "Run the first third of a race with your head, the middle with your

personality, and the last third with your heart.”
This quote by Mike Fanelli encapsulates the simplest, best way to run a race. It's helpful to start a race logically at your goal pace. Don't go out way too fast - think it through.

The middle third of a race can be run with your personality - this means whatever is most comfortable for you. That could include:

- Staying on your goal pace.

- Running faster than goal pace.

- Sticking with a group of runners near you.

Then when you reach the final third of the race, you run with your heart! Pour your soul into the race and see what your body is capable of doing. You might just surprise yourself.

27. Never attack a hill from the bottom during a race.
If you run a long hill, running fast from the very bottom isn't the best strategy. You're going to fatigue yourself and not be able to recover as quickly as you should at the top of the hill.

A better strategy is to run the same effort during the first half or two-thirds of the hill (even though your effort is the same, your pace will slow down). Then during the last half or third of the hill run hard to match your pace on flat land.

When you reach the top of the hill, put in a surge. This is definitely an advanced move, but if you can manage a 10 - 20 second surge at the top of a hill you'll definitely lose any other runners around you. Save this for when you're not racing with friends!

28. Move your arms quickly when running uphill.
In a race, time is money. Hills present a big obstacle and can dramatically slow you down. To help yourself get over the hill without losing so much momentum, imagine that you're throwing pebbles at your feet.

This simple cue will keep your arms pumping - which helps your leg turnover stay high.

29. When running in minimalist shoes, it's OK to go a little slower.
You may feel light and fast, but running in minimalist shoes at your normal
pace is often too fast. You're putting added stress on the tiny muscles in your
feet that aren't used to being activated and used very often. Any time you add
a new stress, it's best to do it gradually.

Running slower than usual helps limit the impact forces you're exerting on
your feet. You'll be able to run with better form and be more mindful of how
your legs feel with significantly less shoe on your foot.

30. Give running a rest. Go multi-sport!
Sometimes, you just need to take a break from running. The best way to do
this - and still stay fit - is to train for a multi-sport event like triathlon (swim,
bike, run) or duathlon (run, bike, run). Both sports allow you to continue
developing your endurance while experimenting with new forms of exercise.

You'll also be able to increase your athleticism by working different muscle
groups and prevent injuries by getting stronger and correcting imbalances
that form through consistent running. Triathlon or duathlon training has you
running less, but you'll likely be working out even *more*.

When you eventually come back to only running, you'll be a stronger (and
faster) runner.

31. Are you a new runner? Stop those long intervals!
Long repetition interval workouts should be avoided by most new runners.
Stick to short sprints, easy distance runs, and tempo workouts. Beginners
need to focus on opposite ends of the running spectrum (easy and very fast)
to develop their general endurance and ability to sprint.

Those long intervals (like 1200m or up) at 5k or 10k pace put a stress on your
body that new runners aren't ready for yet. After about six months of
building your fitness foundation, you can start more race-specific workouts
that are progressively more challenging.

32. Know the race course before you race.
For a long road race of 10k or more, know the course before you arrive. It's
helpful to run it beforehand during a long run or drive it in your car to
understand the turns, terrain, and hills that you'll have to run on race day.

At the very least, study the course map and also the elevation profile (if available) on the race's website. Knowing where the aid stations, restrooms, hills, and major turns will help you better plan your race strategy.

33. Plan your splits before the race - then run your plan.
Before the day of your race, determine your goal time and break that down into mile or kilometer segments. Knowing your splits ahead of time can help you stay on track and pace yourself accurately on race day.

Most races will have markers at every mile or at least at important check marks along the way - like the 5k and 10k mark - so you'll be able to tell if you're running too fast, too slow, or just right. And then you can adjust accordingly.

34. Periodize for important goal races.
A lot of runners will read this and not understand what I'm talking about so let me explain: "periodizing" your training is simply shifting the priority of your running over time to focus on different things.

Almost all training programs should have three general phases: base, specific, and sharpening. Let's go over each one:

· The base phase prioritizes endurance and sprinting (but *not* hard workouts). Your goals are to build your mileage base, incorporate a lot of strides or hill sprints, and run aerobic workouts like tempo runs or easy fartleks.

· The specific phase is simple: the workouts start to resemble your goal race. As you move away from general mileage and neuromuscular work (like strides), you move closer toward interval workouts like 5 x 1,000m at your goal 5k pace with 1 minute recovery. This workout is very specific to a 5k race.

· Finally, the sharpening phase is also called a taper and focuses on rest and making sure your body is 100% ready for race day. Your workouts will typically be faster than race pace, but shorter.

These training phases allow you to gain endurance, get fast for your race, and then recover enough to have a great performance on race day.

35. Run workouts that that have more than two paces.

Common workouts among runners include a set of intervals at a predetermined pace like your current 5k or half-marathon pace. There's nothing inherently wrong with these workouts - in fact, they can be great during the specific phase of your training period.

But including 2-3 *different* paces in your workout can help you learn to run faster when tired, boost your fitness, and improve your finishing kick. So instead of your next 3 x mile at 10k pace, try the following:

2 x mile at your goal 10k pace with 3 minutes jog recovery, then 2 x 800m at your 5k pace with 2 minutes jog recovery.

This workout has you running at a faster pace at the end with the same overall volume. Hopefully this workout will help you negative split your 10k race!

36. Run harder on your hard days and easier on your easier days.
Most runners run a "medium" effort on most days. They go out for their run and run "their pace" for the entire duration of the workout. This strategy doesn't take advantage of the adaptation cycle; there's a better way!

Make your easy days easier by running less and running slower on those particular days. But an easy day is best if you also take care of yourself by using your foam roller, taking an ice bath, and getting extra sleep. And when it's time to run hard, make sure you don't slack off! Your body needs to be pushed to get faster.

37. Stop fretting about your VO2 Max.
It seems that every runner who is serious about training is obsessed with their VO2 Max score - the maximum amount of oxygen that your body can transport and utilize during exercise. Sure, VO2 Max can increase with training, but it's not a good indicator of how fast you'll be able to run on race day.

Some runners have a really high VO2 score but poor running economy (efficiency) so they're slower. Other runners are the opposite and run significantly faster. The lesson here is that there are better things to focus on - things that you can actually control in your training - so don't worry too much about your VO2 Max.

38. LT is more important anyways!

Your LT is your lactate threshold. This is the point at which your body transitions from working aerobically (with oxygen) to anaerobically (without oxygen). It's marked by a significant increase in breath rate and the familiar "burn" of hard running.

Lactate threshold responds better to training and you can improve it more easily than VO2 Max. Your overall weekly mileage, long run distance, and tempo workouts have the most effect on your LT and should be important components to your training plan.

39. It's not all about the tempo.

Sure, tempo workouts are incredibly valuable and you should incorporate them regularly into your running if you want to see results. But there are other race paces that work really well to increase your endurance and get you fit.

Your half-marathon and marathon pace are also great paces that will boost your aerobic fitness. Each should be slower than your tempo pace, which is about the pace that you could manage for a full hour. Both will help you increase your ability to run faster - and further - without going into oxygen debt.

40. Practice race pace.

It doesn't matter what race you're running, you need to practice running at your goal race pace during training if you want to achieve your time goal. Only running intervals at faster than your race pace and easy running isn't the best way to get in ideal race shape.

Instead, plan your workouts so you're running about the same distance as your race at your goal race pace. A good example workout is 5 x 1,000m at your goal 5k pace, with a 400m recovery jog in between each repetition.

This workout is very specific to the 5k race and will give you a good indication of your fitness level. Once you do a few of these types of workouts, you'll know if you're ready to run your goal pace for the entire race.

If you're not sure how to plan your workouts, I can help with a custom training plan that's personalized to your running history.

Running Gear

Running apparel and accessories don't just help you stay comfortable when you're out running - certain pieces of gear should be used as tools to help you become a better runner.

That's what this section is about. You won't find any particular gear reviews, but instead you'll learn how to use the right gear to improve your running.

41. Stop buying such expensive shoes.
Dr. Bernard Marti, the leading preventative-medicine specialist at Switzerland's University of Bern conducted research that showed the most common variable among injured runners wasn't training volume, the intensity of workouts, or frequency of races. It was the *price of their running shoes*. Runners who paid more than $95 for their trainers were more than twice as likely to get hurt.

Expensive running shoes tend to have all the bells and whistles: a very elevated heel, lots of motion-control "technology," and plenty of "shock guidance systems." They haven't been proven to help you run faster or keep you healthy, but you'll sure pay extra for them.

Stick to shoes that are generally in the $80 or less price category. They tend to have fewer motion-limiting features that tend to increase your risk of injury.

42. Occasionally wear a pair of minimalist shoes.
Wearing minimalist shoes for all of your running is probably a bad idea. Most runners don't take enough time to transition gradually and safely - and they end up hurt. A better idea is to wear a lighter, more flexible shoe for 1-2 short and easy runs every week. You could also wear them for your weekly fast workout once you're used to the easy runs in minimalist trainers.

Wearing "less shoe" will help you develop stronger lower leg and feet muscles while reinforcing good running form. It's more difficult to aggressively heel strike in light shoes so you'll be forced to run more economically with lighter, quicker steps.

43. Wear flip flops in the summer instead of sneakers.

It seems that every runner who's been to a specialty running store has heard about the benefits of barefoot running and wearing lighter, more flexible shoes. But that's not the only way to reap the rewards of stronger feet.

Instead of focusing on your running shoes as your only source of minimalism, your casual shoes can play a big part in developing foot strength as well. Flip flops are a great way to get your feet on a level surface (no heel lift) with little to no arch support. Just be careful not to take any long walks on your first day or two wearing them; you'll need some time to adjust first.

44. Wear Sperry Topsiders at the office instead of bulky dress shoes.
Just like with flip flops, you can work on your lower leg strength with minimal stress at the office too. If your job is a little more casual, Sperry Topsiders are a great pair of minimalist shoes you can wear daily.

They're essentially boating shoes but look great with a pair of khakis. If your office is a bit more formal, try driving loafers. They're just as low to the ground, flexible, and have a minimal heel lift.

45. Keep a training log.
As the wise saying goes, "What gets measured gets managed." Besides being a valuable learning tool, you'll be thankful that you have records of what you did every day later in life. Talk about a helluva heirloom for your grandkids!

You can choose to use a hard copy training journal - any notebook will work - but there are also online options for you. Websites like www.dailymile.com or www.runnersworld.com/log are very popular. And of course, a plain old Excel spreadsheet works fine too.

By using a training log, you can look back at your training to see how you were able to run such a fast race or find the errors in your running that led to a poor performance. If you don't have the past records, how will you know?

46. Change into a pair of minimalist shoes when you run track workouts.
One of the most beneficial times to run in minimalist shoes is when you're running fast. This is an advanced technique but will help you build foot and lower leg strength to help you prevent injuries. You'll also reinforce an efficient running stride, helping you improve your economy.

Remember that this is an advanced strategy so if you're not comfortable with racing flats, spikes, or other minimalist shoes you should first start by running easy in them. Once you're ready to wear flats for a workout, do your warm-up and warm-down in your regular trainers and reserve your "fast shoes" for the fast portion of the workout.

47. Do you wear cotton socks? Get rid of them!

There have been a lot of innovations over the last 25 years in performance fabric. Your grandfather's tube socks just aren't going to cut it these days. To prevent blisters (the #1 reason runners quit ultramarathons) and chafing on your feet, you need high-quality socks.

Try socks made from synthetic material like polyester to help wick sweat away from your skin so it can evaporate. Even better, products like Wright Sock combine two layers of fabric (don't worry, they don't retain heat) so if there's any rubbing, it's on the second layer of fabric and not your skin. Your feet will thank you after your next long run.

48. Invest in a foam roller.

Muscle soreness and tightness after a long run or workout are common (and of course, desirable for the adaptation process). Sometimes it can be helpful for some self-massage with a foam roller to help speed the recovery process.

The fancy term is "myofascial release" and it simply means massage. It can help loosen tight muscles, promote healing blood circulation, and break up scar tissue and soft tissue adhesions. A foam roller can also be used to release tension caused by trigger points – particularly tight spots that are tender to the touch.

You can do some rolling before you run as part of your warm-up. Just make sure you keep the pressure lighter than usual so you don't make yourself sore. After you run, you can be a little more aggressive.

49. Use a tennis ball for self-massage.

If your foam roller can't get deep enough on bigger muscles like your hamstrings and glutes, then you can use a tennis ball for more targeted massage. It can be especially helpful for those trigger points in your muscles.

Unlike a foam roller, a tennis ball can make you quite sore if you overdo it.

Try to keep your self-massage time to 3-5 minutes per muscle to limit the chance of it making your muscles overly tender.

50. Wear compression socks.
Compression socks work! They can help you recover when you use them after your run or for long periods of time when you're sitting. They can also be helpful for minimizing damage during long or particularly hard workouts or races.

When purchasing your compression socks, make sure that they're *graduated* - meaning they're tighter at the foot and ankle than up near your calf. They can be hard to put on and take off, but the benefits are worth it!

51. Heart-rate monitors don't make you faster.
Too many runners think they need the fanciest gear to help them get faster. Heart rate monitors aren't necessary to be a good runner, but they can be a useful training tool for a more advanced runner.

There are two specific types of workouts that lend themselves very well to heart rate training: recovery runs and tempo runs. It's important to make recovery runs truly easy so a heart rate monitor can keep you honest and make sure you're not working too hard.

Tempo workouts are typically run at about 85-90% of your maximum heart rate. You can use a heart rate monitor to determine your max heart rate and then work at the correct percentage. It may not be completely accurate, but it can be a valuable tool to help inform your workouts.

52. Want a home gym for $20?
Gym memberships are expensive. The average person pays about $500 annually to belong to their gym and more than half of people over-estimate how many times they'll visit the gym when they first sign up.

Instead, get a 10-12 pound medicine ball. You can do a full body workout in ten minutes by doing simple exercises like lunges, squats, dead lifts, chest press, and ab work with a med ball. Many exercises can be done standing up - perfect for runners who should be doing some of their strength work while standing (it mimics the demands of running).

The Runner's Diet

You can be a good runner whether you eat vegetarian, paleo, or "traditional." There are certain ways that you can optimize your diet to promote better health as well as improved performance.

The demands of being a distance runner require a few changes to a more conventional diet to help you recover and stay healthy. Follow this advice and you won't just be healthier, you'll feel better and probably run faster!

53. Stop eating processed foods.
We've heard it before - but how many of us have *actually* cut all of the processed foods from our diet? The vast majority of us haven't. Processed foods are loaded with simple sugars, too much salt, an abundance of empty calories, and likely too much fat.

More insidious than just the garbage you're eating, is what you're *not* eating. If your diet has a lot of processed food, then it's displacing a lot of nutritious food that you should be eating. By not eating the vegetables, quality meat, nuts, and fruit that you should, you're starving your body of the nutrients it needs to recover properly and perform at your best.

54. Consider eating paleo.
If you need a short-term diet to get your weight down or prove to yourself that a "diet" doesn't have to feel like a diet, consider eating paleo. This means is that you avoid all processed foods, grains, and most sources of carbohydrates.

What's out: pasta, bagels, rice, quinoa, chips, donuts, bread, and other sources of carbs.

What's in: fruit, vegetables, healthy fats like olive and coconut oil, high-quality cuts of meat, seafood, nuts, and the occasional starchy vegetable like yams.

You'll avoid blood sugar highs and lows and likely lose a lot of weight. Just keep in mind this is an unsustainable diet if you're running a lot - you need more carbs for higher volume running. But it's a good short-term solution for weight management.

55. Take this challenge: eat vegetables at every meal for a week.
We all know that we need to eat more veggies. But aside from the serving of vegetables we have for dinner, most of us don't eat as much as we should. For one week, challenge yourself to eat a serving (or more!) of veggies at every meal.

Here's a sample menu to get you started:

Breakfast: scrambled eggs with chopped mixed vegetables, topped with salsa and avocado. *Optional:* Put it on a bagel or piece of bread for a great home-made breakfast sandwich.
Lunch: Salad with olive oil based dressing, chicken, and a V8.
Snack: Carrots dipped in almond or peanut butter.
Dinner: Steamed broccoli, fish, sauteed eggplant, wild rice.
Snack: Ice cream (go wild!)

56. Have a specific post-workout recovery snack planned.
And once you do, stick to it. Getting on a consistent refueling schedule is important to make sure it becomes a habit. Right after a long run or fast workout, take in some simple carbs, protein, and some more complex carbs to help you recover quickly.

My favorite post-workout snack is a protein shake with whole milk and a piece of fruit. If I've run particularly long or hard, I'll add some chocolate syrup to the shake. Luckily, my stomach can handle the whole milk and the extra calories from the fat aren't an issue for me, so it works well. Experiment with energy bars, mini-meals, or shakes to find your perfect recovery fuel. For some, chocolate milk works best.

57. Embrace your coffee addiction.
Coffee (caffeine) improves running performance - plain and simple. It fundamentally changes how muscles function, making them contract more quickly and forcefully. It also changes how you perceive running-related fatigue and "pain," allowing you to run faster before you start slowing down.

Aim to consume about 1.5mg of caffeine per pound of bodyweight about an hour before you race or run a hard workout. This is about 10-14 ounces of standard brewed coffee. Just make sure you're accustomed to coffee's effects on your GI system before you try it before a race (coffee makes you go to the bathroom, in case you're not aware of this).

The only thing that can be unhealthy about coffee is what you put in it. Be wary of artificial sweeteners, use only as much sugar as you need, and opt for whole milk as opposed to flavored creamers which usually have a lot of chemicals in them.

58. Stop eating so much sugar!
The majority of runners think they need a lot more carbohydrates than they actually do. Unless you're running a marathon in 1-2 days, you don't need a bagel, bowl of oatmeal, and an energy bar after your easy 4 miler.

Most traditional sources of carbohydrates simply add empty calories to your diet that only stimulate an unneeded insulin response. You likely don't need all the carbs - they're just accumulating around your waist.

59. Cut back on the booze.
If you're a drinker, try to limit your alcohol intake in the evening before bed. Women should cut themselves off after one drink while men can typically drink two standard servings. Alcohol will make you fall asleep faster but then it disrupts your sleep and prevents you from getting restorative REM sleep.

Without getting this type of deep sleep, you're inhibiting your recovery from training (not to mention getting dehydrated). Another benefit of slow-wave Delta sleep (very similar to REM) is that this is the important time when your body secretes Human Growth Hormone. HGH aids your recovery and helps repair muscles - but your body makes a lot less when you skip this sleep stage after a night out on the town.

You don't have to be a member of the clergy, but learn to pick your battles when it comes to alcohol. Choosing to prioritize recovery during hard training might make the difference between reaching your goals or falling short.

60. If you're a vegetarian, pay extra attention to your diet.
For vegetarianism to work for endurance athletes, you have to consistently monitor your diet and make sure you're getting the nutrients you need to optimize your performance and recover properly.

Vitamins B6 and B12 (crucial for energy and recovery) are often limited in vegetarian diets and difficult to absorb. Getting enough protein (important to rebuild your muscles) also requires additional care when planning your meals. The best advice I've heard is to include some protein during every meal and take Vitamin B supplements.

61. It's ok to cheat on your diet every now and then.
There's no harm in cheating on your diet once in awhile! You may not be on a real "diet," but more of a "healthy eating plan." Regardless of how you eat, any diet that's too strict will feel confining and you'll want to cheat way more often.

But when you let yourself cheat on occasion, you feel more flexible. Do you really think all of the hard work and discipline you've shown over the week will be flushed down the toilet by a few cookies Friday night? Live a little!

Just make sure it's an *occasional* cheat and not a regular indulgence!

62. Eat more healthy fats.
Healthy fat contains a lot more Omega-3 fatty acid chains than less healthy saturated fat. These healthy fats have been shown to reduce inflammation and your chances of obesity, heart disease, and diabetes.

You can get yours with avocados, nuts, cold water fish, and olive oil. Start eating 2-3 servings per day and you'll probably improve your blood panel while feeling great!

63. Drink a variety of teas.
Tea? Yes, tea. There are a ton of beneficial nutrients in tea, antioxidants that help you recover from running by fighting free radical damage. Many teas have also been implicated in preventing cancer, heart disease, and even diabetes. Some studies have even showed tea's ability to lower cholesterol and prevent dementia.

You don't have to get fancy with many of the high-end, loose teas available at specialty tea stores. Try a variety - here are my top recommendations:

· Green

· Black

· Yerba mate

· White

· Oolong

All of these teas contain caffeine so make sure you're not super sensitive to the effects of this stimulant. If you're not a coffee drinker you can use tea for your pre-race buzz!

64. Run fasted once in awhile.

Occasionally run in the morning without breakfast to practice running on low glycogen stores. A moderate effort in this state has been shown in studies to help you burn more fat instead of carbs and make you more efficient with your existing carbohydrate reserves.

This strategy is a bit advanced, so only experiment with it if you're an experienced runner and training for a longer race like a half-marathon or marathon. A smart fueling strategy can help you achieve your goals in these long races and fasted runs can help.

65. Make sure your sugars are topped off before you race.

Especially before long races of 10 miles or more, eating some simple carbs can help improve performance. These fuels are rapidly turned into sugar and provide plenty of fuel to help you finish strong.

Aim to drink 4-6 ounces of an electrolyte drink (like Gatorade) in the final hour before you race. You can also eat a gel or similar fueling product about an hour before you run. Experiment with what foods agree with your stomach before the day of the race so you know what you can handle. Then go run fast!

66. Eat more cold water fish.

Cold water fish like wild salmon, sardines, or herring have a lot of healthy Omega-3 fats, lower your triglyceride levels, and have been shown to reduce your risk of heart disease. In fact, "Ultramarathon Man" Dean Karnazes eats wild Atlantic salmon multiple times per week and attributes his good health to this diet.

Balance the types of fish that you eat and try to eat two servings per week. The nutrients in fish help fight inflammation and restore fatty acid balance in your body. Most Western diets are deficient in Omega-3 fatty acids and cold water fish is the best source of these valuable fats.

67. Can't eat fish? Take fish oil.
If you don't have a good source of cold water fish near you, there are always supplements. Fish oil is widely available at grocery stores or online and can give you some of the benefits of a diet rich in cold water fish (though, unfortunately, not all).

One of the best sources you can take is cod liver oil. Not only does it have high levels of Omega-3 fatty acids, it is also a good source of Vitamin A and D. It's a little more expensive, but ask your doctor if this type of supplement is right for you if your diet lacks fish.

Recovery and Injury Prevention

Consistency is the key to continued improvement as a runner. But if you're injured and can't run, that's going to derail your training. Making post-workout recovery and injury prevention a big part of your running is crucial to long-term success.

This section will discuss massage, sleep, general recovery, and how to maximize your chances of staying injury-free.

68. Get enough sleep.

For some people that's 9 hours a night. Others work best on 7. Whatever works best for you, stick with it. Sleep is when your body recovers both mentally and physically from your daily activities

Skimping on sleep has the same effects of drinking alcohol: reduced judgement, reaction time, and reasoning. Plus, you won't be recovering properly from your workouts. Adaptation and fitness gains happen when your body repairs itself while at rest. It's just as important as the actual training, so sacrifice sleep at your own risk!

69. Design the perfect night's sleep.

Creating the perfect night's sleep isn't difficult; you just need to learn how to take advantage of what your body wants. First, make your room pitch dark (blackout curtains might be helpful). Next you may want to run a small fan for some white noise - this is especially helpful for folks living in an apartment building. A high quality mattress will also help you stay comfortable and asleep with as little tossing and turning as possible.

Before you even go to sleep, don't watch TV or use your computer up until the time you go to bed (the blue light from the screen screws up your circadian rhythm). If you must use your computer, use a program like stereopsis.com/flux that changes its light output to stop mimicking sunlight. Finally, read fiction for 20-30 minutes before going to sleep. You'll sleep like a baby.

70. Get off the roads!

I'm being dramatic. There's nothing inherently wrong with running on the road, but every runner can benefit from trail running. With a softer surface, trails can help you recover faster from hard workouts. The varied terrain also helps you build more coordination and work more stabilizing muscles.

As a junior in high school, we had a cross country captain who mapped a handful of trail runs on conservation land in our town over the summer. During the next season, we did almost all of our runs on these trails and had a helluva lot more fun than our old training runs. Getting lost in the woods (physically and mentally) is therapeutic.

The Kenyans always say that "roads kill fresh legs." They do almost all of their training on rolling, dirt roads. There's something to be said for the rolling terrain that helps them train consistently – it's easier on the body and builds more strength. Move a few of your runs every week to the trails instead of the roads. The sounds of birds and leaves are better than traffic, right?

71. Vary your training!
Stop doing the same distance, in the same shoes, at the same pace, on the same damn running route every other day. The body thrives on variation and it can help you avoid injuries since you're not putting the same exact stress on your body every single day.

You can insert more variation in your training by rotating 2-3 pairs of running shoes, running different types of terrain (trails, hills, roads, etc.), and changing the types of workouts you do every week. Make your easy days easier, your hard days harder, and don't forget to do a variety of strength and mobility drills to keep your body moving in different planes of motion.

72. Stop stretching after you run.
Instead of stretching after your runs, try a dynamic flexibility routine. Stretching *dynamically*, or while you're moving instead of just holding a stretch for a period of time, is more effective at helping you warm-down and recover from a run. In fact, studies have shown that static stretching doesn't help you recover at all.

Dynamic stretches can include leg swings, hurdle drills, lunges, and leg raises. This is my favorite dynamic stretching routine (which is perfect for a warm-up - but more on that later): http://strengthrunning.com/2011/07/the-standard-warm-up-video-demonstration/.

Of course, a *little* bit of static stretching after your run is just fine and if you think it makes you feel better, then keep doing it. Just don't spend longer than about a minute on each muscle.

73. Stop stretching before you run.
Stretching before you run is actually harmful. Not only will it decrease your running performance by reducing your muscle power, but you'll be at a higher risk of injury. Who wants that?

It's best to spend 5-10 minutes doing a set of dynamic flexibility drills. Just like the "Standard Warm-up" routine mentioned previously, a good mobility sequence will help you literally warm up, increase blood flow to your muscles, improve your range of motion, and get you physically ready to run.

One of the best investments in your running is to include a warm-up routine of dynamic stretches. You'll not only run faster, but you'll feel better and be more resistant to injury.

74. If you're tired, run slower. If you're sore, run slower. If you're both, consider taking a day off.
Runners need to be intimately in tune with their bodies. Learn to recognize your early warning signs of fatigue, soreness, and pain. When you're experiencing all of them, you may need to skip your scheduled workout and focus on recovery. As Dr. George Sheehan said, "Don't be a blind and deaf tenant."

Remember that your body gets faster when it's able to rest and "absorb" the training you've already done so don't be shy about resting when your body needs it. The best workout for you is exactly what your body needs on that day.

75. Don't ice bath after every hard workout.
Instead, save ice baths for your easy days or after occasional hard workouts. See, when you do a fast workout or long run, your body is probably going to experience some soreness. This is a *good* thing because then your body repairs itself, adapts to the new stress, and ultimately gets stronger. Why would you want to limit that adaptation?

Ensure your easy days focus on recovery by adding in an ice bath (or just a regular session of icing). It's a great way to help your body recover without reducing those necessary training adaptations.

76. Take a down week.

A "down week" (or a recovery week) in your training is when you reduce both the volume and intensity of your running to allow your body to recover from all the hard work you've been doing. These are especially valuable if you're putting in more miles or harder workouts than you ever have before.

A good way to schedule down weeks is every 3rd or 4th week. An example of a typical marathon training week for you might be 35 miles and 2 workouts. In a down week, you'd run 25 miles and only 1 slightly easier workout. Make sure to truly take advantage of this recovery period by getting extra sleep and eating a healthy diet to give your body what it needs to repair itself!

77. Take an easy day every week.

That might be a day off or just an easy jog. Depending on your fitness level and ability, it's helpful to have one day (or maybe even more) to completely focus on recovery and rest.

Here are a few options, from easy to advanced:

· Take the day completely off from working out.

· Take the day off from running, but do 10-15 minutes of light core or flexibility work.

· Take the day off from running, but lift weights at the gym.

· Take the day off from running, but cross-train with cycling, pool running, elliptical, or swimming.

· Run an easy run of 20-45 minutes - keep the pace slow.

78. Take naps.

I'm not recommending that you get lazy, but naps are a valuable tool in the runner's recovery toolbox. Pro marathoner Ryan Hall calls them "business meetings" and they help him recover from the hard workouts and mileage that he puts in before his races.

Naps that are ten minutes or longer have been shown to have significant mental benefits like improved alertness, memory, and motor learning. The real napping powers come into play when you nap for 60-90 minutes.

These naps speed recovery and allow your body to rebuild from your workouts. That's because these longer naps include slow-wave Delta sleep and REM sleep cycles, which is when your body gets flooded with Human Growth Hormone (HGH) - the best recovery aid that you could ever wish for.

79. Beware of the office - move around!

If you have an office job, stay loose throughout the day. Sitting in the same position for 8+ hours is not only bad for your general health, but you'll be creating muscle imbalances and decreasing your range of motion.

Here are a few ideas that can help you stay loose throughout your day:

- take frequent walk breaks

- use a standing work station

- sit on an ergonomic chair (or Swiss ball)

- don't call your colleague; walk to her desk

- take the stairs

- print to the far side of the office

- have standing meetings

The options are endless; just make sure you alternate your positions throughout the day and keep moving around.

80. Staying healthy is about more than injury prevention, it's about preventing colds.

When you can limit the number of colds you get throughout the year that means you'll run more consistently and take less time off because of constant illnesses.

To stay healthy, use these simple tips:

- Eat probiotics (very important for immune function) daily with yogurt or Kombucha Tea.

- Don't skimp on sleep!

· Avoid processed food - when you do, you're probably skipping healthy food.

· Stay hydrated.

· Eat your fruit and vegetables.

· Don't be obsessive about washing your hands - your body needs some exposure to normal germs (but don't be gross either).

Staying healthy doesn't have to be hard or expensive, just follow the common sense ideas above and you'll likely stay a lot healthier next cold season.

81. Don't tie your shoes so tight.

When you pull your shoelaces as tight as you possibly can, you're restricting the movement of your shin muscles and tendons where they attach to your ankle. Sometimes shin splints can be caused by too much pressure on the tendons on top of your foot.

There is a lot of personal preference to this issue but if you're having foot, ankle, or lower leg pains then try loosening your shoes slightly to allow a little more flexibility. Just make sure they stay on your feet!

82. If you're going minimalist, strengthen your feet first.

Jumping into a pair of minimalist running shoes and starting your next run isn't the best way to make the transition if you're new to "barefoot shoes." Before you do that, it's best if you prepared your feet and lower legs by doing a few specific strength exercises first.

There are three effective foot strengthening exercises that can be done while you watch TV. The first has you scrunching a towel with your toes. Lay the towel flat and scrunch one end so you roll the towel closer to your leg. Do ten reps. For added difficulty, place a large book on one end to give yourself some resistance.

The next exercise is picking up marbles with your toes and dropping them in a jar. Put 15-20 marbles (pebbles work too) on the floor and pick each one up with your toes, drop it in the jar, and work your way toward 3 sets of 20 marbles.

The last exercise is simple: wrap a rubber band around all five of your toes and then splay your toes to the side. Do three sets of ten reps. After a few weeks your feet will be a lot more ready to run in minimalist shoes.

83. It's ok to take a day off every now and then.
I'm as guilty as every neurotic runner who hates to miss a planned run. I crave structure! But sometimes it pays to relax and skip a run. The world won't end and you won't lose any of the hard work you've already put into your training.

The mental benefit of skipping a workout far surpasses the physical benefit. Sure, you might get an extra hour of sleep and feel more recovered. But *mentally* you're refreshed and rejuvenated. You're reinvigorated to start training with more enthusiasm. How much is that motivation worth?

84. Plan for rest and relaxation.
Every runner needs down-time (yes, even pro runners take weeks off and don't run a step) from regular training. Extended periods of 1-3 weeks of zero or very low-mileage running can be quite beneficial - both mentally and physically.

Your body needs time to recover and rebuild. Your mind needs time to get excited about running again. When you plan a few weeks off from running a few times every year, you'll feel better about your running and ultimately perform better in your races.

Plus, it's more fun to go through periods of intense focus and planned laziness. The body works better in pulses.

85. Run gently.
Sounds simple, doesn't it? You'd be amazed at how many runners I see on a *daily* basis whose feet are aggressively striking the ground. If your feet are slapping the ground loudly, you're increasing your injury risk. The increased impact forces from a hard foot strike will cause more muscle trauma in your feet and lower legs - and even make you more susceptible to stress fractures.

Focus on landing gently with your feet underneath your center of mass. Just think: if you can sneak up on a dog, you're doing great!

86. Give yourself an ice massage!
Sorry, this type of massage isn't as fun as the one you get at the spa. To ice a

sore part of your leg, freeze water in a paper cup. When it's frozen, tear off the top 1-2 inches to expose the ice and use it to rub the sore muscle.

This is a more active method of icing and allows you to get deeper into a muscle and apply pressure to the affected area. Since you're applying ice directly onto your skin, limit your icing time to ten minutes to prevent your skin from getting too cold. Nobody likes self-inflicted frostbite.

87. Take an ice bath.
Ice baths are a more intense way to help you recover from an especially hard workout or long run. A good way to get used to them is by using a cooler or bucket and filling it with water and ice for your lower legs. Once you can do that without screaming (good luck), you can take a full ice bath.

Fill your tub with cold water and dump 1-2 pounds (3-4 if you're crazy) of ice in the water. Strip down to your running shorts and hop in, sitting in the tub with your legs straight. Stay in the tub for 10-20 minutes. That's an ice bath! You may want to take a warm shower afterward to warm up.

Bonus reason to take an ice bath: cold therapy like this has been shown to be just as effective as medication at treating depression.

88. Never go to sleep tight.
Sleeping is your best recovery tool, but going to bed when you're already tight (say, from sitting for hours) won't maximize the recovery you'll get from sleeping.

Instead of just crawling into bed at the end of the day, do a short session of dynamic drills to loosen up. Just a few minutes of leg swings and other flexibility exercises will help your legs recover faster - plus, you'll feel better in the morning!

Motivation and Random Training Tips

Not everything fits into a neat category, so the final section is a random assortment of lessons I've learned to help you dominate. Everything from selecting a doctor, increasing your motivation, and goal setting is included here.

Do you have more suggestions? Email me at support@strengthrunning.com!

89. Don't be afraid to run in the heat and humidity.
Those brutal summer runs might be slow, hot, sweaty, and miserable, but they actually help you. See, your body learns to be more efficient when the temperature and humidity are really high. You lose less salt through your sweat and better regulate your body temperature. In fact, high heat training can actually simulate running at altitude.

Of course, I'm not recommending you give yourself heat stroke during 100 degree days in the middle of summer. But with 1-2 moderate runs every week in hot and humid conditions, you'll improve your body's metabolic efficiency. Just remember to hydrate!

90. If you're struggling to reach your goals, get a coach who can help you dominate.
Coaching isn't just for elite athletes anymore. Runners who want to find more focus, stop getting injured so often, or get faster in an upcoming race are looking to coaches who can help. With a custom training plan built specifically for you and regular communication about your workouts, it may be just what your running needs.

The internet has made coaching affordable and accessible to anybody with a computer. If you're wondering if a coach is right for you, keep in mind that you'll have to be a good communicator and like interacting online.

If that's you and you like what you've read so far, I have several coaching options available for runners: http://strengthrunning.com/coaching.

91. Make sure your doctor is a runner.
Having a doctor who is a runner, cyclist, or other endurance athlete can make a *big* difference. It's helpful when they understand why you run so much,

why you *need* to get in your run every day, or your abnormally low heart rate.

A doctor who runs will also be able to refer you to better specialists who can help you rehabilitate an injury. I've had doctors tell me that "the human body is not built for running longer than 5 miles," so it's helpful to have one who knows what you're going through.

92. Chase a seemingly impossible goal.

Maybe it's qualifying for the Boston Marathon, or running an Ironman Triathlon, or even breaking 25 minutes for 5k. Whatever it is, commit yourself to it with vigor.

Big goals don't get accomplished overnight so dedicate yourself to it and stay committed. Remember, the best time to start was yesterday. The next best time is today.

93. Read all you can about running.

Nobody likes information overload, but you should learn as much as you can about running so that you can tweak your own training and become a better runner. When you understand a little bit of the physiology of running and how it affects your body, you'll be able to respond to your body's signals and design training that will make you a much faster (and healthier) runner.

Resources like Running Times magazine and common books available can help you understand more about the sport of running. For the full list of running books I recommend, check out my Runner's Library resource.

94. Learn to like running in bad weather.

An unfortunate reality of being a runner is that you have to run in all kinds of bad weather. If you live through all four seasons that means heat, humidity, rain, wind, mud, brutal sun, cold, sleet, snow, and ice. Maybe that treadmill is starting to look like a better alternative.

But running outside is more specific to races - the last time I checked none were held on treadmills - and a helluva lot less boring. As long as you have the proper gear and take the necessary precautions during poor weather, you'll be fine running outside.

As Bill Bowerman, former head track coach at Oregon and founder of Nike once said, "There's no such thing as bad weather, just soft people."

95. Set achievable goals (in addition to your monster goals).
Little, achievable goals - or "small wins" as I like to call them - help you stay motivated and boost your confidence. Staying motivated to run and train will help you reach your goals dramatically faster than if you didn't maintain a positive outlook.

Two of the best ways to regularly have small wins in your training is to negative split easy distance runs and to run "mini-workouts" - or shorter versions of more traditional workouts. Both can be done during any part of your training and neither requires a high level of fitness. Give them a try - you'll like the results.

96. Pack your bag the night before a race.
Who wants stress on race day? Instead of frantically searching for last minute items like anti-chafing cream or your favorite socks, pack it all the night before so you aren't late to the start.

Also consider a few other conveniences for race day:

- Print directions to the race (or have the route mapped on your smartphone) so you have them handy.

- Set two alarms just in case one fails.

- Prepare your breakfast the night before.

- Leave your house earlier than you think before the race.

97. Use the buddy system.
Train with a runner who's at a similar fitness level to help you stay motivated and push you to run faster than you normally would. The normal competitive instinct will turn on and you'll improve more quickly. Just be careful to not push each other too hard on your recovery days.

You should also convince them to race with you. You can push each other to run faster since you know exactly how fit the other person is. Many times improvement is purely mental - a running buddy can help you get over any mental hurdles you may have.

98. Run the tangents!
Too many runners run *longer* than they have to in races. See, a race is

measured by finding the shortest distance from the starting line to the finish line. That means running the tangents - or the shortest distance between two points.

If you're running around a curve, don't stay on the far outside of the road and run a wider turn than you have to. Stay close and run tight. In longer races like the marathon, running the tangents during every turn adds up to a significant amount of time.

And nobody wants to race longer than they have to!

99. When you're feeling low on motivation, watch something inspirational.

Everyone gets disillusioned with their training once in awhile. Maybe you're not excited to do a particular workout or your low on motivation after a poor workout. You need to get your mojo back so you can get back to running!

Here are the best ways to get excited again:

- Watch a pro athlete run an impressive race or workout on YouTube.

- Read a few inspirational running quotes (here are 19 of my favorites).

- Explore a new trail or running route - get out of your routine!

100. Carry ID when you run.

Carrying some type of ID with you is smart. Just in case something happens to you while running, first responders will know your name and where you live.

A product like Road ID goes a step further and allows you to customize an ID to include a phone number, email address, or even allergy information. You can wear it on your wrist, shoe, or as a necklace.

It's a small precaution to take to protect yourself in case something awful happens and you can't speak for yourself.

101. You don't have to use a seven day training calendar.

Most runners plan their training in seven day cycles. It's the most convenient way to do it because there's seven days in a week. Scheduling a Monday and Wednesday workout, Friday recovery day, and Sunday long run has been a staple for thousands of runners.

But it's not the only way to plan a good training program. You can also use a ten or even 14 day training cycle depending on your goals. If you're an ultramarathoner, it might be more beneficial to run long runs every ten days or two weeks. Some runners may need more recovery, so they should schedule three hard workouts per 14-day cycle.

There are a lot of options available to you so don't think that one-week schedules are the only way to plan your training. If you're not sure where to start - or you'd love some guidance - I have several coaching options available to you.

102. Run with a partner.
A running partner is valuable in many ways - to both help your training and motivate you when your will to train is low. Find a friend, colleague, or neighbor who has a similar ability to you and you both can motivate one another to run more, race faster, and enjoy the sport.

You'll also be able to learn from one another and discuss your running goals, how well you're improving, and any injuries that might come up. There's power in numbers so don't discount the importance of training with other runners!

The next best thing is joining a community of like-minded runners online who can inspire your training. Find a forum, website, or training group of runners and you'll find people with similar goals who are more than happy to support you.